ART OF MIND II
....
ALL IN

BY ORIGINAL CLYDE AIDOO

Copyright © 2012 Original Clyde Aidoo
All Rights Reserved.

ISBN: 0615547028
ISBN-13: 9780615547022

Library of Congress Control Number: 2011917645
CreateSpace Independent Publishing Platform
North Charleston, South Carolina

No sharks were jumped in the making of this sequel.

*FOR THOSE
WHO CAN'T FIND THE WORDS*

Not everyone can afford to
go on a shopping spree of assorted degrees —
Education isn't always earned — sometimes it's simply paid for.
Some may not be legibly gifted,
or Do have the words, but just can't lift it...
Some shout ideals and make passionate appeals,
but no one hears them:
Because they have No Voice.
Even I may be among the latter, so this
is for those who have felt what I felt, and *feel* what I felt
— and may feel again.
My pain was no stronger or more poignant,
Only theirs may never be heard —
Just because they can't find the words.

Ruffled Clouds Inc. Presents...

Another Philosopoem Collection...

In Association with RPRP Publications...

Editing by
Clyde Aidoo

Artwork Provided by

Robert Beck
Dian Bernardo
Bruce Braithwaite
Vincent Cacciotti
Yashmin Campagne
Chet Davis
Luis Ludzska
Cynthia McBride
Aixa Oliveras
Minako Ota
Kate Owens
Eric Palson
Bonnie Shapiro

Written, Spliced and Produced by
Original Clyde Aidoo

Art of Mind II
All In

By Original Clyde Aidoo

CHAPTER I

IT HAS MY HEART, BUT IT LOOKS JUST LIKE YOU

Thank You

"Thank you," he said, with a still expression and tears in his voice.
Sincerity soaked in those two small sponges, and it was the shower of acceptance —
or Love — or both — that befell him and he used to absolve himself.
She acted unaware, but she knew what he was thanking her for.
I've heard the same phrase spoken by fallen angels who were picked up when they thought they could never stand again…they showed gratitude in their loving eyes and frequent appreciative strokes. But in case that wasn't enough, they say, "Thank you."
They package their delivery with emotion so those two little wings will travel farther, but in case that isn't enough, if asked to explain their message, tears often escape the silently quivering voice and spill down towards their lips.

"Thank you" — it's a phrase said so often in passing, it's often taken for granted.

Patrons to Servers

Recipients to Delivery Men

Checkers to Baggers

Customers to Clerks

Clerks to Customers

Owners to Visitors

Strangers to Strangers

The Clumsy to the Generous.

The same two words for handing down dinner rolls are expressed in this much more profound instance. Those two words alone can't be depended on, so they're emphasized with deep, earnest stares and soul-measured tones to ensure the full message was received.

It is usually dropped long after / / And Before a specific act of kindness. Just a "small" "Thank you." Those who have said these Thank yous know to what I am referring...

and so do their recipients...though they usually insist on acting surprised.

I am not too proud to say, "Thank you,"

but they usually leave before I have a chance to tell them.

So when faced with an Eternal Dilemma:

Either continue falling deeper into a dark hole, or take it all as it comes...I decided it wasn't much of a dilemma.

Can't say that I'm happy... nor content... but I am something a bit Easier:

I'm at Peace.
There may come a time when I am faced with that
Dilemma again…
Then again,
I could actually become Happy.
Until then, I'll keep grinning,
Someday, I may even start smiling.

I am proud to have come this far on my own;
but I'd much rather have someone to thank.

Those Who Are Lucky

We like to say those who are lucky
Don't realize what they've got,
And how good they've got it...
But what if they did?

What if they bragged about their many conquests?
What if they posted pictures of their adventures
with Numerous Women?
What if they gave veiled advice meant
to boast their sexual adventures
more than to boost the listener's odds?
What if they committed every ounce of their being
to express the pleasures of the flesh
In Their
Music,
Art,
And every conceivable platform of pop culture?

What if they held hands for all to see...
With a tender stare
Without the decency
to look away?
What if more free time is spent on the telephone than
with the outside world?
What if the expression: "I love you"
Is not whispered?
What if they spent
Every Waking Hour
of

Every Single Day
In the company of their companion?
What then?
What *Now*?

So here is my message to Those Who Are Lucky:

Thanks for reminding us.

It Has My Heart, but It Looks Just Like You

Every birth begins with
Crossing Eyes
&
Meeting Paths.

This Creation is no different.

Your passage left me deeply departed.
I tried to travel through those tubes,
Then I couldn't bear the sight of your hegira.

The only things swimming are expectations,
down a barren, sterile tunnel.
My lips never touched yours.
Seismic timing interceded between an
Atomic Love Encounter.
Detached alienation didn't help, either.

It may seem a miracle, but
something was conceived that day.
Seeds were planted.
Deep-Rooted & Home Brewing.
Until embryonic molecules spread between these
cells.
Fostering, Circulating,
Emerging.
Isn't it beautiful?
I don't need to carry this for nine months.
Don't need paternity leave.

IT HAS MY HEART, BUT IT LOOKS JUST LIKE YOU

I can keep popping them out.

Congratulations, we've got centuplets.

I've been impregnated by so many
Hard-Boiled Legs & Over-Easy Teases,
I wouldn't be so quick to take credit for this.

Sorry, you are *not* the mother.

She thinks she left me empty,
but together, we created something special.
If it wasn't for her, my drive would have stalled...
and now...
I just keep on pushing.
I don't need a birth coach...
My labor has brought life to this.

I'll take this newborn home,
Then make another without hesitation;
Although it has My Name,
For less than $20 —
I'll Share Visitation.

CHAPTER 2

ETCHED

Unsung

It's sad how narrow a voice can travel,
Even with the Range of a Soprano —
Just because so many doors are closed.

There's only room for so many Divas...
You can belt your heart out and shatter glasses
but you cannot crack Ear-Muffs...
You're a superstar blending with the rest of the masses,
It seems that's just tough luck.

There's a voice as pure as Norah's,
With a pitch that cannot be made clearer...
Yes, Somewhere — there is Someone Singing:
And No One is around to hear her.

Fear of Large Crowds

They say that
Two's Company
&
Three is a Crowd…
That's why it only takes One Fan —
To truly make me proud.

You're No Ted Danson...Keep Waiting by the Door

It's good your
Inspiration
Is so widely-known,
If inspired by fiction or a no one —
That could land you in a padded home.

So I hope you get
three
Cheers,
And lots of fortune and fame,
In order to inspire the world —
"Everybody must know your name."

Etched

It takes more than ink to be etched
into stone. To be engraved one must be graved —
Even if not gravely missed. Though one's demise alone isn't
the surest way to rise, rather one must simply be really, really old.
To be centuries older than the oldest man alive is the surest way to stay alive.
Indeed a measure of greatness is to continue to stand above all upright feet with no detectable contender amongst the millions of weary contestants. Or is it just a sign of the times? Not these times — *those* times. Times where you could write your own ticket to immortality while you were still alive. And when you *did* die? Well, your verse wouldn't go rotten, because their archaic language ages like fine wine while
I'm
Sippin' on this forty ounce,
Seems we're standing on the corner as
The same names are re-announced.
Shakespeare was a baaadd dude but he can't be Badder than Michael,
Wordsworth's words couldn't hit harder than Ali,
Sweet Emily wasn't more loveable than Lucy…
And while none of the latter names are replaceable, seems they are quite comparable:
Ushers are put on the same stage as Michael,
Tyson takes a bite out of Ali's Greatness,

And Lucy's tenured rule seems overshadowed by Shows about Nothing and Reality TV — not to be confused.
It seems that only moving images can budge the wheels of time, while those with pens are etched in stone. But it *does* take more than ink to be etched in stone. It takes timing. Seems we're hundreds of years off.
Maybe the revered names of yester-century will remain unchallenged because they're so much more talented than I will ever be.

Fair enough.

But if *I* don't speak to the nation, then I know Somebody has to.
Someone who writes for the people and not a false sense of belonging amongst the kitsch niche with hollow awards and fustian circles that won't let the world in.
There has to be Someone only writing and not rapping who is worth enough to have his wallet read, "Bad Mother Fucker."
If you want to reign over shelves today you have to be a "King,"
Alongside maybe a couple "Pattersons" or "Robertses...." but hey at least they're today…
But that's just fiction. Where does that leave us with the trippy talk?
Can one of us be the next Shakespeare? Or is that just poppycock?

No one is above comparison,
No matter how important,
Some even say Kobe is the Greatest,
Though Clearly he's no Jordan.
Seems if you really want to be remembered, you should stay in school after-all. Learn how to write your hearts out, because as long as you're on screen, the channel will eventually change.
If you want to be the best for decades and centuries to come without being contested by names of today or even a few years back,
Just jot ten timeless poems or so…
There's only just One Catch:

It must be a Billion Years Ago.

CHAPTER 3

HOURS IN VOLUMES

Hours in Volumes

Days shouldn't feel this empty.
Sealing capsules without substance lowers already knocked off pedals of will —
halting locomotive chains that were
barely moving anyway.
I'm still expected to approve the dross and waste of a full 24 hour rotation,
and send it out as if completed, and as if ready to begin anew the following day.
How can I? How can one be satisfied with a malfunctioning vacuum of winnowed pieces
that cannot be out-placed?
A Day's Quality has managed to evaporate once more,
so I must now settle for a quantitative mass-producing of
Hours in Volumes.
Deep-Sixed Ticks rise from a deserted grave

and I succumb to its strangle, until my body slumbers,
but No —
I Will Not Rest.

A Salesman's Omission

"Go out and Live!"
Exclaims the world!
They sell the notion of
Living Every Day
Like it's the last
and to not let a single minute
Be lost.
With a drowsy eye
and a wavering head —
I sit up in my bed,
and skeptically ask:

"How much does that cost?"

The Thoughts of a Man in a Dark Room

The curtains are open,
but my words are already drawn:
Now the room has trapped the darkness.
The mind composes a requiem of cadavers, cartilage,
and carcasses already reeking from the perfume of
wretched doom...
These recordings aren't to be played for the family:
These thoughts are of a man
Entombed in a Dark Room.

Out of the Dark

You don't hear any
Whimpering from Me,
Now there's a certain
Peace when I Sleep —
No ocular strain or needed sheep…
Isn't that how it's
Supposed to Be?

CHAPTER 4

BLANK STARE

Me Against the World

Never take your eyes off the opponent...
Any great will tell you that.
Even before the bell...
Tyson was the best at that.
I'm alone in the corner.
Eyes on opponent.
Always on opponent.
I pace, loosen, stretch, waggle.
They may remain steady
or step violently in an attempt to intimidate.
My eyes shift with them.
Where they go, my eyes follow. Every movement is countered by my head.
My focus is undaunted, unflinching.
Finally, we meet in the center.
Human rulebooks stand in-between...
Telling me what I can and can't do.
I pay no attention.
I stay focused on my opponent.
I make no faces —
No menacing gestures.
I just stare.
One of Tyson's victims swayed during the staredown...
Trying to stay active and keep his energy.
Tyson's head remained firm as Iron,
but his eyes swayed with the opponent.
Left to the right. Right to left. His eyes followed.

I go back to my small corner
where no one can touch me.
My opponent has already been announced.
The match already set.
It's Me Against the World.
Bell rings.
I leave my corner in pursuit of a partner.
A Formidable Tag Team Duo.
Together let's win the title; Change the title:
Us Against the World

The Staredown

I'm not used to being looked at that way.
Rather, I'm not used to having someone around *to*
look at me that way.
No, no, it's just *that* look.
There was a certain admiration, lust,
Power
In her stare...that proved just too much.
Now I can stare down Bloods & Crips,
Starving Nymphs,
Navajos, Ball Pros, and Hos...
but it is honey and sweet things
that bring the Strongest Men to their knees.
When she wins this staredown, she may assume it's
because I'm weak —
When she really is just oblivious to her own strength.

She engages me with that look.
That tender, longing look.
I step up to the plate —
Ready for whatever she throws at me...
Then my eyes go like the electricity:
Down and Out.
And our hopes go like a
Bambino slug:
Up
Up
&
Away.
<sigh>
I inhale, Man Up and Look Up...
But as I looked away —
She had gone away.

Blank Stare

Her eyes rise.
She gives a seductive glare.
But until she knows what she's eying —
This is just a blank stare.

The physical scope is far too limited,
Her lens can't expose what really matters.

I know what she doesn't know about herself —
Which is that she knows nothing at all.

Her eyes are dancing and her lips are curling —
Very inviting, not very exciting.
Because I know until she gets to know me,
Our slate is clear and will likely remain unwritten.
I'm an *outsider*, different, perhaps even unusual,
I'm willing to bet this type isn't her usual.

I wish I could say I don't judge by covers,
but she seems fairly easy to read.
I'm nearly certain I know what she goes for,
and I have the good sense to know it ain't me.

So her smiling and staring is empty —
Since it means Absolutely Nothing.
If I am wrong, by all means
sit with me:

And let's get to work —
Filling in these blanks.

CHAPTER 5

FIRST IMPRESSIONS

First Impressions

Go on. Strip me down.
I hope to do the same to you.
Look to exploit any vulnerability or fears,
I hope to be around to take *yours* away.

Pick away at any fault, any verbal trip-up, and keep looking for *any* weakness;
While
I'll keep building you up:

Using *all* your strengths.

The Habit

I've got this terrible habit, you see.
I could go my entire life having never heard of something —
And granted, it's been out for a while, as in years, but it's sort of hidden
Somewhere among all the others.
I mean, like her for instance…she's been around for over twenty years,
and I hadn't the slightest clue…
But now I do.

I can't seem to control this habit.
It can be a popular primetime show that I never watch,
A made for TV movie that is average at best,
or it could be anything attention-grabbing that I just happened to run into unexpectedly…
Like Her.
All of a sudden, all the time I lived in oblivion no longer matters.
What matters is that now I'm tuned in,
And she has my full attention.

And my day cannot resume until I see what happens.

You see I got this terrible habit:
It doesn't matter how little I knew of her existence…
Once I saw her,

I knew I had to
Keep Following —
and
Find out the Conclusion.

Keeping Distance

Wait. Wait Right there.
Just keep waiting.
I'll come to you.
I'll extend my arm,
Even open my heart.
I'll do All the Work,
And say All I need to say...
The only thing I ask in return:
Is that you
Meet Me Half-Way.

Pitching without an Agent

He's had multiple movies to keep your watch.

He has a portfolio of prints to earn your stare.

He has a trunk full of songs to win your
Unconditional Admiration.

They've had many chances to win your thoughts —
With the whole world as their agents.

If you would give me One Listen with the
Same Attention
that you give to them...

We would be Famous.

13 Seconds

She probably thinks I do this all the time.
She couldn't be more wrong.
Somehow, I think that if she knew
How special these seconds are,
She'd probably reconsider.
She probably thinks it takes any curvy backside to make my tendons spasm.
She probably assumes that all it takes is beauty to prompt such an unselective approach.
Maybe she's right.
Maybe I'm delusional.
But I can swear I can see inside,
And it only took 13 seconds.

I may follow her steps for minutes to confirm this sighting,
and when I'm certain of what I see —
I know what must be done.
She probably thinks I do this all the time.
Who could blame her?
But the truth is after this encounter, I will return to the sidelines.
Seems I'm Running out of Downs,
And I May Never Go For It Again.
I'm going to be inbound for months,
Sometimes it feels like years.
And the tragedy of it all,
Is no matter what I say,
She thinks it's only her outbound beauty,
And she thinks I do this all the time.

CHAPTER 6

SILENCE AND STONES MAY BREAK MY BONES, BUT WORDS WILL NEVER HURT ME

Standing Rejection

No one likes rejection,
but the worst that can happen
Is you'll wear a frown…
Do not Fear Making that Stand:
Nobody Has Died
from being
Shot Down.

Fourth Degree Murder

Let things go their natural course,
Stop getting in the way,
She can make her Own decisions,
We can do without your petty say.
As she drags her friend away,
She could be pulling away destiny,
How can that whole group think it's ok?
One should have the guts to bring her back to me.
Sometimes it's only one Blocker,
Weighing no more than a Buck Thirty,
The target I want has her Guard Down,
But this Center is Playing Dirty.
Who knows what could have been?
Maybe a child or even a family of five?
All it takes is One Senseless Act —
To stop fantasies from Growing Alive.
I'm trying to do "Right By Her"
Still I'm being abused more than
Tina Turner…
They Think they are Saving a Friend,
While committing
Fourth Degree Murder.

Silence and Stones May Break My Bones, but Words Will Never Hurt Me

She might not smile as much as you,
Won't be mistaken for a humanitarian,
But she admits to eating men alive,
While you claim to be a vegetarian.
She's no Miss Congeniality,
Doesn't wave, or play to the crowd,
But she'll tell you when the hunt is over,
While you lead on a lost Blood Hound.
Some may think that she's stuck up…
Since she doesn't take part in false pageantry,
But at least she will tell a Dog —
When he's barking up the wrong tree.
You see, silence says a Thousand Words,
And she has only said a few…
She had the courtesy to tell me, "No."
I can't say the same for you.
You are loved by many…
Your people skills keep a crowd around,
But when One Guy wants a little closure,
You suddenly can't produce a sound.
The whole world is convinced that you're sweet,
While Ms. Blunt has to take the heat —
For being real when she could have been quiet,
You blame your conscience on brittle chicken feet.
And if it's true that you were afraid…
Then I think we both can agree:
You were clearly considering yourself,
So don't say you were considering me.

The only difference between you and her:
She was kind enough to say, "Kick Rocks..."
They call her a Stone Cold Bitch,
but You are the Real Ice Box.

CHAPTER 7

DEAR HUNTING

Second to Ass

Keep on being that nice guy,
And no, you won't finish last...
You'll always be in better standing
Than an Ass
Who
Doesn't Get Ass.

Check Your Status

Welcome, my brother.
Yes, I share your pain.
I relate to your loneliness,
Your longing for companionship,
Your desire to be loved.
I feel ya. Trust me, I feel where you are coming from.

Who's she?

Oh, an ex-girlfriend.
What's that?
You dated her for three years?
Oh. That must hurt. Let it all out, man.

I feel ya. Trust me, I feel where you are coming from.

And her?
Oh ok.

I heard about your party. They said it was another epic.
Maybe I'll come over some time...
If I can find the time.

Oh she's cute...
How do you know her?
Oh yeah?

Yeah. HA HA! You're right. He seems like a cool guy.

But wait, I know you're down and out,
And it's not like it's some competition,
But I just couldn't help but notice —
All this activity is a weekly repetition.
Well, look, man, I'm just saying...
It's not that I'm saying you're a poser,
It's just that a lot would kill to have it like you,
So you might want to change your composure.
If you think this is sad — that's depressing,
Because your life seems to look just fine,
For someone who claims to be lonely,
Your door sure revolves a lot more than mine.

Dear Hunting

I know far too well what it's like to be frustrated at the prey for being so damn elusive.

They can be as sly as a fox...
When all you want is to catch you a Dear.

You get in position.
And you lie in wait.
Prepared to strike.
You think you're equipped with everything you need...
But you forgot
It takes Game to make her your Game.

Maybe you have on too much camouflage...
She *must* not have seen you judging by how she passed you by...even after you approached to go in for the kill.

Instead of re-evaluating your methods...you're quick to put the blame on the prey...
Like any frustrated hunter: you swear out loud when you don't get your way.

You call her a bitch, a slut, a picky stuck up cunt...
My dude, don't blame her,
Blame Nature...
It ain't *her* fault that you
Don't know how to hunt.

CHAPTER 8
NO WAY SHOULD IT BE THIS EASY

Just Another Physical Prodigy

I couldn't get over that girl with the sweats.
The girl with modest make-up.
The plain pony-tail...
She was just as beautiful as the girl with the dress.
Yeah, I liked the girl with the sweats.
The girl with the moderate makeup.
The pell-mell ponytail...
Yeah, I liked that girl.
That girl was Mine.
Not "Mine" Mine, but, you know...
Mine.
It wasn't until you slipped on that dress,
When you stopped being just "my" girl,
It was much easier to get over you,
When I knew you belonged to the world.

That isn't to suggest you're suggestive,
I just couldn't believe you're such a
Hot-Commodity...

When I thought you were scarce I had regrets,
Now you're just another Physical Prodigy.

Let's not give too much credit to the outfit,
To be honest, it's just how you look today...
You see, I thought I had a chance,
Now I see that there was No Way.

When you cut me off, I thought I did wrong...
I thought I must have owed you a sincere apology,
But now I Understand:
You're just another Physical Prodigy.

No Way Should it Be This Easy

You deserve better than this.
You deserve to be immortalized in the shrines of minds and wheeled through Grapevines, not left behind as if you're not the best find I or he will Ever find.

Inhale.

After you left me shattered then separated I have the nerve to forget your clumsy touch. I don't care that you dropped me, I feel blessed that you even touched me. Now I'm fighting to keep your memory alive without your

Body *or* Mind here to Remind what Time we had shared, yeah I know you didn't care, it's not like I was your significant other, just a quite insignificant other — who you left behind and moved on to another but I don't want any other — I want your memory to haunt me so why the hell is it so easy to breathe these days when you're not here to choke me with your dismissive words or fleeting transitive verbs?

Exhale.

They say Pain is what lets us know we're alive, but that's not why I can't let you go; see the trouble is I find my resolve slipping, when I say, "I Can't Let

You Go." I don't care about the pain or "feeling alive" or any of that crap...hell, to be honest, I don't even think I want you anymore because a man has his pride and all...I just want to remember every word and most of all I simply want to remember your face. I don't know, I guess I've always been a believer in people getting what they deserve. And

That's What You Deserve.

The Way I Looked At Her

You may not be Her,
but
I will not do to You
what
She did to Me.

If you could see how I looked at her,
It would only make you feel small,
Then after seeing how you look at me,
I wonder what I ever saw in her at all.

I guess it was her eclipsing beauty,
Her shining personality,
Her philanthropic nature,
Her lucent smile,
Not sure if I mentioned her personality...
but *God.*
Yeah, just that.
But you're ok, too.
Really, as long as you give back whatever I give you,
As long as you look at me the way I looked at her,
If you can match that look then I'll know how you feel about me.
And I won't make the mistake she made:
I won't take that for granted.

You may not be my first pick,
But I'm glad you're on my team.

I'm willing to see this thing through.
And who knows?
Maybe you'll see that look after all.

CHAPTER 9

CLOSURE

General Hospital

No, I don't watch "soaps,"
I usually watch just one...
I only wish I had been watching
from the day the show begun.
Man, that would've been sweet!
To have been watching from the start!
Well, I guess there's always YouTube —
To recapture "Faces of the Heart."
Some states it airs at 3,
In mine es numero dos...
Me Habla Espanol —
for Sonny Corinthos.
By that I mean no homo,
Don't take it the wrong way...
A grown man watching daytime —
Doesn't make him gay.
They say it's unrealistic,
The over-acting they can't take...
When did they last tune in?

I find *this* acting fake.
The emotion is "over the top,"
So many tears and so much drama,
No chance of misconception,
No exemption or exception.

The whole genre lacks respect,
but I'll still stay in General Hospital…
And if someday I terminate my stay —
I'll Always have
One Life to Live.

(R.I.P. January 13, 2012)

The Recast

Am I really that replaceable?
I thought that my dreams finally
Came to Fruition,
Only to find out I barely made
The Audition.
Damn, can I do another take? You haven't heard my best stuff!
Can I change 'drobe
in case I look a bit rough?
Because I know I'm my own kind,
I just need one more take to try and
Change your mind...
Instead you just move right on, only shouting,
"Next!!"
I'd move my Whole Life, and you can't even text?
I know you can find another, that's of no surprise,
That doesn't mean you have to be so quick
to
Cut Off All Ties.
I thought I'd be the Man on Fire to your Dakota Fanning,
I should have known we're all replaceable
When they changed Todd Mannings.
I mean Howarth was Primetime, even on Daytime —
His fans will always remember,
Most others don't.

If someone that Unforgettable can suddenly be
Erasable,

Right there I should have known that
We Are All Replaceable.

On May 13, 2011, Roger Howarth returned to One Life to Live as THE Todd Manning. Thereby providing new hope for all us replaceables.

So Much for My Happy ---

The first approach is a hint,
A second would be a slight give-away,
But once he confides in another and discusses her in a conversation,
That's when you know.
Yep.
That's when you know...
The guy will get the girl,
And they will fall in love.

Boy, if only real life were that easy.

I'd cast my leading lady cautiously,
Someone worthy of a fairy tale.
It wouldn't matter how I approach,
She won't care. Not in the long run.
Because eventually, somehow,
I'd do something or say something...
We'd bump into one another at some fortuitous and chancy occasion.
You know - - like Serendipity.
Somehow, someway, it would all work out in the end.
Fate will Reveal and Prevail!
Strictly because I want her that bad.

Now why can't it be like that?

Why are we only given one chance?

And why does one of the two always care so little
about fate —
No matter how blatantly obvious it is?
And for the love of all things sacred —
When can we finally answer the age old question:

Why can't the good guy win?

We could have had a True Love Story,
Even though I'm sure you knew what was pending,
Instead — you left me Incomplete...
Well, So much for our Happy

Closure

A friend of mine once told me that
There is no such thing as closure.
When they're done, they're done,
That's It,
It's Over.
It'd sure be nice if it was more like the Soap Operas.
I don't mean the yelling and the drama and the throwing stuff...
It'd be nice to know that you'd see that face again, and that whatever is meant to be —
Will Be,
And whatever happens — there will be closure.
It'd be nice to saunter aimlessly about town and end up on a pier at the same time the woman on your mind is just standing there, looking out into the water...all by herself...
With Absolutely No One Else Around.
That'd sure be nice.
To have that kind of timing, and for it to be out of our hands.
Only in real life this never happens, instead the weeks go by as we await a phone call from the one who has to deep down recognize the error of their ways...or at least have the courtesy to discuss their conclusion.
But the phone never rings.
I'd like to just take a walk through the park in an empty town designed only to unscramble empty

pieces and puzzling endings and find the same
woman a week or so later. Once again. All by herself.
And not even be like,
"Oh my God. You again!? What are the odds!?"
But just simply state,
"Hi. How are you?"
All...Matter-of-Fact Like.
Then we'd pick up where we left off at the pier.
And if it must keep happening at the park, or the
same pier over and over again, or best yet — an
empty bar, that's my favorite...then so be it. It will
continue to happen because in *this* world, our
guardian angels refuse to let us go out like that. They
will see to it that we get that closure we so richly
deserve.
And after everything is finally out and settled...
suddenly, that park, the pier, and the only local bar
in town suddenly become even emptier...or much
more crowded.
And the face is gone as it should be.
Like a relationship purgatory that didn't know where
to go, but is now finally wherever it belongs, and out of
your life.
It may be awkward at times, but it'd sure be nice to
have a little closure. To find out what went wrong
without always being the one to pick up the phone.
Or better yet, to say an amicable goodbye and
sincerely reflect on memories one last time.
Yeah, that would be nice.
Almost as if thinking about the other person wills it
into happening.

CLOSURE

If it were like that down here, then
I would've seen her Every Single Day…
Until there was closure.

I don't think I'd be the only one.
Those parks would be as packed as Wrigley, those
piers as crowded as Navy, and those bars would have
Capacity Met
Yes, yes, yes, it'd be Nice to have just a little closure.
But that's why it's a Soap Opera.
Because here in this lonesome town:

The Phone Never Rings.

CHAPTER 10
HANG-UPS

I Could Hold the Best Conversation

I Could Hold the Best Conversation!
Record Milestones
Like the Couples Do...
I don't need to ever Get Off —
As long as I can tend to you.
I'll listen like no one has —
Before you know — Three hours pass...
Your voice really revs me up...
That's why I'm far from being out of gas.
Gabby Blondes, a Rambling Lush —
Ellen Degeneres, Craig Ferguson...
Had I not been so out of practice —
I could've held my own with anyone.
I Can Hand Hold the Best Conversation!
I Know I Can, I Know I Can!
I did when I was Growing Up,
So I know this mouth can Yak Again.
Do not be fooled by my reticence,
I'd be glad to offer my two cents...
Once I'm rid of these distractions —
This void will fill interactions!

Lunchroom Conversations,
Picnics with familiar relations,
Pick the occasion or the setting:
My attention Spans
Parks to Serengeti.

I'd Rule the Art of Conversation,
Clyde's not in, it's "Your Royal Highness..."
This Call I Cannot Answer,
because My Life Rings of Awkward Silence.

Hang-Ups

Now Just Hold On!
See this is one of my
Biggest Hang-Ups.
I know this started Ambivalical,
That doesn't mean you should Cut the Cord!
Ok so I made up a word,
I can still put a sentence together!
But once you cut me loose then we can
Never get back together.

You say you have unlimited minutes —
So why are you only giving me five?
You and I both know, "I'll call you right back,"
Translates to, "That conversation was whack."

Let's ride this stormy weather,
Then maybe we'll learn to love the tide,
And once we get through this,
We can come through to the other side.

All the Way

I'm so used to interacting through servers,
I thought I'd never hear your voice.
Feels like it's official now:
We have finally connected.

Thank you for helping me break down these *Walls*
Though this is hardly first base, I'm already hoping to go All the Way.
I don't care how many miles, or how much the flight costs:
I'm willing to go All the Way.
Just show me the way — I'll follow.

Now I don't want to lose us by getting ahead of myself…
This one conversation is enough confirmation
of our connection.
Though I may never feel your touch,
Hearing your voice means so much.

We may never book a flight, or prompt a
Domestic Airline Confirmation…
But I *feel* this Heavy Connection —
This was a Real Friendship Consummation.

Unread

That could be anyone I want it to be: Just as long as I don't look.
What a Wonderful World This Would Be:
If instead of family, a club promotion or a common acquaintance…
It was actually you.

My phone vibrated,
It Took the Text:
But I'm still not ready to receive it…
Until it's Proven it wasn't you:
I still have reason to believe it.

CHAPTER 11

W W I

WWI

Now dis is gunna b a cumplete n total disasta
Sumbody clear da roads cuz Im only gunna go fasta
Yall kno i keeps it real cuz
I neva knu how 2 act
So wen i say dat I am faded den
im trippin here on dis cognac
U aint readin wrong
dis aint no shyt 2 b investigated
Dis is my tru confession: i am

Writing While Intoxicated.

Yo brigade aint shyt imma run rite thru dem 2
N after I tank dis poem den
Im aimin rite at u
Dey said dis was mission impossible
But im cruisin on thru dis shyt
I allready took 6 shots
N still droppin anotha hit

N droppin bombs 2
Becuz im fully equipped
im blowin dis shyt up
and damnit im havin fun
ok i admit
dis is worse den

World War I.

well I did say dat dis would b a total disasta
sumbody died while readin dis so can sumbody
plz call dey pastor
aw shyt I gotta go
im bein told to pull ova
but whats scarier den dis?
Sum Ppl write lyke dis

When They're Sober.

Fort Neva-Should

Private, you don't belong in this Army!
No, really, you really don't...
Sure, you'll get to see a lot,
But there's so much more you won't.

Before you decide to enlist,
I have a Unit of Reasons
To List:
Why you should stay stationed
at Home,
Instead of a place with a corked
Time Zone.
It isn't 13 Hundred,
It's simply One O'clock...
This is the type of nonsense —
That gets a private shot.
But back to the mission at hand...
You have to understand:
Once that chopper lands —
You're in a Top Secret land.

Private, this isn't the Standard.

Foot Hikes, PT,
Combative Sergeants —
Even
IEDs are the least of your Worries...
When you leave your body will detach —
From the limbs of Contemporary.

You'll miss so much that you can't get back —
Like time with family and things you won't see:
Births, Graduations, Weddings…
&
LeBron James joining the Heat!

Survive in My Shoes

If I ever wonder how some people would react in my shoes:
I need only to look at the military.
Some people don't know what to do when they are cut off from the world,
which is why any sign of contact they have...they clutch it as tightly as they can. See in the military they're trained to guard their every possession with their lives...they learn to take accountability for letting *any* valuables get away.
I've felt cut off for most of my life...even though admittedly I've been a very free man...
but when some are cut off for less than three months...
They're already ready to Leap.

I maintain my discipline and composure,
While they think they're in love, I know it's a phase...
They were in my shoes for Only Two Months:
Then lost their minds & got engaged.

Drill Sgt.

I don't think you want to be free.
If you did you'd just walk on out.
Instead you Choose to let him run your life.
I don't think you want to be free.
Maybe you should join the service.

It must be nice to have it like him,
To shout orders and receive total discipline.
He knows that even when you shout back: You will never leave —
Especially if it's in writing.

You've chose to serve him for over four years,
And Now you're choosing to Re-Up?
Re-Up? You Crazy?
Re-Up? You out of your Mind?
He manages to squeeze in a few proud or sincere moments a month,
and of course that makes you even more fond of him.
I'm not sure how he does it.
He treats you like dirt and clearly puts Specialists ahead of you…
and still you keep coming back.
I just can't figure out how he does it.

He must really know how to handle Privates.

Well,
maybe *I* should join the service,
And work my way up to be Drill Sergeant,
That way I could do as I please —
and Know you would Never Leave.

WWII

Come One! Come All!
Welcome to my
Merry Car-Ni-Val!
I'm not just slayin' you...
I'mma Murder Fuckin'
All-A-Yall!
I'm talkin' 'bout Jokes!
So come in and let's
Have-A-Ball!
When I hit 'n' run
Then that means I'mma be the
Last-2-Call!
But this time I think I'm sober,
So maybe you can make
Sense-of-it-all!
Enough with the intro,
Come on in and join my happy
Free-For-All!

Nevermind.
I'm about to pass out,
You can go on home
After-All.

CHAPTER 12

UNIVERSAL TRUTH

Getting Through

Yes, I got your point,
There's no need to
Keep Talking Louder...
The fact that you are wrong:
Doesn't Change Because You're a Shouter.

Give Up, Dude

"Don't Give Up."
"Don't Ever Back Out."
Let's just be honest:
You need to
Tap The Fuck Out.
Don't stay in a battle
That you can never win,
It Takes Giving Up:
To Live to Fight Again.

Universal Truth

Him on the computer screen:
That guy always speaks the truth.
That guy on the TV screen:
Hey, like him or not, he speaks the truth.
That guy who makes those records:
You know *he* always speaks the truth.
That guy writing those words:
He's so real, he speaks the truth.
The truth of the matter is:
There are Millions who speak the truth,
They may not spit it or wit it like some — But listen carefully,
I'm telling the truth.

Hired Gun

Mother fucker gave you a bad look.

You can't have that.

That ho is mouthing off...

Yeah...shut his ass up.

Son of a Bitch — Took Your Bitch —

You got sumpin' for that...

Dude must have a Death Wish....he's at the wrong place, wearing the wrong colors...

Oh Hell Naw....
You Can't Have That.

It's clear you
Couldn't survive in schools,
So it's good you can survive these streets,
Instead of making these Special Ed Rules,
You could at least Reach for Public Feats.
Don't get so Personal and Attached,
No Assassin can Succeed Like That,
You could become a Paragon of Public Safety,
And use that Gat to Exterminate Rats.
Instead of being a Part of the Problem,
You can Decide to be Part of the Solution,

It's too late to turn your life around,
So here's a better resolution:

Instead of putting the innocent in harm's way,
And ending young lives with more reckless action:
Rid us of Baby Killers and Molesters,
And kill Vermin like Vanessa Jackson.

You may not be the brightest one,
You can't turn back, it's too late for you, son...
So just go up against Greater Evil:
And be the World's
Hired Gun.

Never Underestimate

She will give you all the love she has to give.
She will give you all of her daydreams,
Every minute detail of her day...
She will give you her mind,
Body,
Often her soul.
She will give you her tears...
She will give up her body to you...
Then she will give up her body *for* you.
She is a Nurturer,
A Mother,
A Lover,
A Friend.
Yes,
Never Underestimate the Love of a Woman.

But...

He...Now He...

He hangs on a limb
With Open Arms.
He dreams twice as much about an entity
That he doesn't expect anything from.
He wishes,
He reaches,
He Leaps...
Even though he is nearly certain he will fall.

Yes, He turns a single look into an ignition,
A kiss on the cheek into an explosion,
A Plain Jane into a Fantasy,
A Fantasy into an Obsession.

Yes, he takes kindness and temporary friendship —
And creates a Dream.
He turns passing conversation and one ambiguous sentence
Into the wishful stargaze of a teenager leading into a portal of hope.
He doesn't need flowers, candles, or an already consummated union to act irrational.
He only needs a pretty face to launch into another galaxy.
A warm heart and genuine personality only takes him further…
If not farther.

He is not
A
Creep,
A Stalker,
A Weirdo,
Or
A Loser.

Do not be surprised if he becomes too attached,
I swear some women just don't understand…
You may not feel the same way,
But Never Underestimate
The Passion of a Man.

CHAPTER 13

ART OF MIND: PHILOSOPOEMS TO THE
WORLD: THE GALLERY

Palms and Semi

Trespassing?
No:
I'm paving my own paradise.
I'm making my way through a rainbow field swirling
in a tropical landscape:
Palm trees as high as my imagination can reach,
supported by gold & strawberry red stems.
There are high translucent wires parallel to the trees.
They hang like telephone wires in a secluded
woodland...and above it all is the clearest blue sky.
This makes me feel like Hawaii.
Now I want to go there next.
Or maybe Savannah, Georgia or down the road over
to Miami.
This feeling is unlike anywhere I've ever been.
Feels like open air with only
Silk on the Skin.

I sit alone, only me and these palm trees.
I'm too inspired, and just like those cords
I'm too wired.

I must paint what I feel.
I can't leave this all with me.

Left only with my paint and no paper... I begin to stroke...
I sure hope the owner of this Semi won't mind...
It's the only thing here...so it will have to do.

They too are probably wandering and taking this all in...
I'm sure he or she won't mind.

These up and down strokes begin to blend with the setting,
but now I must take a step back
to look at nature's work.

This scenery takes me away, so I may not return to my modified canvas...
I do believe the owner will not mind...
I'm sure that he or she will see the beauty of it, too.

Painted by Donna Marsh

Fierce Guardian

The wind blows on his dusty mane,
but this guardian remains still.
He has suffered wounds from battles from every
predator and prowler this open jungle has seen, but
he remains in wait — unfearing of another battle,
for he will fight until his last dying breath...and
regardless of the outcome —
You Will Remember He Was There.

He continues to lie in wait.
He will not hunt you down...but he
Will Not Be Your Prey.
He will protect his young, his legacy, and his
territory...
and with weary eye and a feeble heart —
This land *will* bear the markings of a
Fierce Guardian.

Proceed at your own foolish risk.
You'll only grant his last dying wish.

Painted by Judy Gilbert

Over

My suitcases are packed —
But I don't need them.
Not where I'm going.
Although nobody knows where I'm going…
I'm just ready to be free…
I want *no one* to know where I'm going —
But the Good Lord —
And Me.

I've shed the shackles and have done away with my given-name.
I'm ready to take my own fate.
I am well dressed and I am self educated —
I'm ready to climb any hurdle.
I am ready to take on the world —
As a free *man* in a white man's world.

I do not know how long it will take until I get there…
Wherever I am going…
but I can see the sky above my obstacles,
and there ain't no mountain or boulder high enough

That can stop me —
from reachin' it.

Painted by Chet Davis

Blues Queen

She finally made it back to Birdland.
It feels like just yesterday she was here in New York City, spray-painting this bitter, hateful earth with the blues. Now she is on Heaven's replica stage being backed up by the greatest bluesmen that have ever lived accompanying her commanding voice as respective maestros of the
Sweet sax,
Trumpet,
Drums,
A pair of trombones and a double bass:
What a Difference a Day Made.

Oh she's still got it. It feels like Radio City here in the clouds…with flashy lights beaming down on the messengers of song. The stage is overflowing with music and taking center stage is the very physical and spiritual representation of the Blues. She stands before the audience oozing blue, it's wrapped around her skin, and from her soul it pours from her pores… the moment she begins to roar.

She *is* the Blues.

With clenched fists and an open heart — she Rules the microphone…
Victoria and Elizabeth can have their jurisdiction…
But on *this* stage there is but only
One Queen.

I present to you:
The Queen of Blues.
All Hail.

Painted by John Penney

Reflecting Pool

She's on the edge.
Drowning in something
Deeper than Water — She's somebody's Daughter —
But today she's all alone,
Reflecting in a pain that's
All her own.

And I *watch* her reflection.
Just *waiting* for her to fall...
So I can catch her before she sinks —
Into this hole that drains her so:
A suicide angel who's on the brink.

Her curves,
Her reflection —
Are surreal...
I begin to question if she's
Just an Apparition...
I smell a fixation for pain
Floating in the air...
If so
I'm just the man to feed her dark addiction.

Painted by Chet Davis

Artist's Dilemma

This "common artist" is about to ascend
Ten Stories High —

Don't look now.

Now I've reached a place where I'm afraid to fall —

Don't look down.

My art has taken control,
It uplifts me high with an exhilarating view —
But I am afraid that if I choose to let go —
That I'll end up becoming
Just like you.

Do I continue to rise
or
Come back down to earth?

Should I remain alone with only art as my companion?
Or do I release and return to join the rest of you?
I am *so high*
on Fumes.
Still —
This remains a terrifying view.

Painted by Chet Davis

Your Complicated Soul

You are not a pair of brown, soft angled eyebrows hanging above shadowed gray-sky eyes.

You are not a triangular face holding a head of blonde and brown streaks highlighted by hanging burgundy leaks in a room that complements your gentle-orange cheeks.

You are not a pair of delicate, flushed lips or a fair even tone with high cheek bones.

You are neither frail nor fragile.

You are not exposed but you are not covered.

You are not enlightened but you are not ignorant.

You are not a thinly frame in a flowing dark dress.

No, you are not what they think you are.
Though not even *you* know what you truly are.

You are not

weak, not strong, not afraid, not brave,
You are not a girl,
but you are *more* than a woman:

You are a
Magnificent,
Most Complicated Soul.

Painted by Juliette Caron

To Be Continued

CHAPTER 14

AN ARTIST'S EYES

The Art of a Woman

Cashmere skin softer than surah fabric — spun from the very thread of nature…All the way down to their hips — One touch lifts flocculent trips.
Those variety of hips are molded in a feminine lotion —
&
When they move it's
Poetry in Motion.

A Higher Power has created these Models…

And they use His sidewalks as their walkways.

Oh, we stop and stare, because
they have a fragrance about their poise, and an aura upon their confidence.
Beneath those hips lie-thighs with a buried treasure of a potent diamond that uplift new lives upon us.
And with the strength appointed in them they Labor to be Birth Givers,

then perfect
The Art of Caretaking.

Yes a Higher Power created these Models...but they each hold their Own crafted image.
This green earth carries a multi-colored gallery...
With a Maker who disgraces Picasso.

Let us praise His name, for He has done well...
though
I do not know if God is
Male or Female...
I *do* know
He or She

Is an Artist.

An Artist's Eyes

Have you ever looked into
An Artist's Eyes?
If you have then you too have traveled where I have.
You too have been lost in a maze in amazement.
Yes, they are masters of holding another dimension…
Of making viewers
Lose themselves…
They hold mystery and an interpretation left for *you*
to own…
They do it with their hands, their wrists, their
fingers.…
But most of all
I've seen them do it with
Their eyes.

* * *

Have you ever looked into an
Artist's Eyes?
I mean *really* looked?
They are often distant, and somewhere far, far away:
Nestling in a daydream utopia.
Seemingly unaware of this world around them,
yet strangely — also
Taking in Every Detail.
Sometimes I dare ask unexpectedly,
"Are you an artist?"
Why they are surprised that I know — I have no clue.
It's as transparent as water color,

As embedded as acrylic canvas...
It's in their DNA:
They study, they focus, they
train their pupils to dance...
So as I study them:
Boy do they dance.
Together we waltz
As my eyes stare back...
For as much as they study me,
I accept the challenge and
gladly study them, too.
Yes, I know you're away from your canvas,
But I hope you still take requests:

Paint me a picture expressing more than words.
Leave me guessing with the most abstract of glances.
Take me away with your imaginative stares...
And stroke my soul without brushing my fabric.
Yes, *leave me* with a lasting impression...

And P.S:
Keep wearing your own eccentric neo-fashion.

I applaud their wardrobe — then return to their eyes:
&
They gladly meet my requests.

The Antique

I already knew you were beautiful,
But when I saw your photo I did a
Double-Take.
Your lines blur what's beneath,
But now I see you.
The Real You.

I am elated to capture the beatific movement
of this antique stilled image
and carry it on with me every time I see your figure.
And all the aging hours that I don't.

This isn't a slight at the current model,
She's a Beauty, Too.
This was snapped a long time ago,
But It Is Still You.

I did not know of your total beauty,
And as long as you are alive:
That beauty is still inside you.
So
If I'm in a hurry to peel off your layers,

I just want to get close to it.

CHAPTER 15
FINAL SAY

Final Say

Year after Year,
Day after Day,
Beautiful Faces
Keep
Fading Away.
They display photographs of famous faces
That I no longer recognize.
They memorialize images of common people that I have never seen.
The late are displayed the same as when they departed,
and the same with the living elderly, even if a celebrity.
Sometimes I notice that middle age is not far ahead and prime not far behind.
But what I Always seem to notice
In All these photographs:
Are beautiful faces that have faded away.

Each photograph is so up to date...
Of course it *has* to be up to date...
Right?
We must show them as we remember them,
Not as they may wish to be remembered.
They must display the most recent of what remained,
but If they Really want to be Post-Modern:
Why not show the Remains?
If that representation wouldn't be fair,
Why any different than when they've lost their hair?
When selecting the image
to remember them by,
Do not automatically start from today:
Let's give Them a Say.

If I could address the media — during my Last Rites,
I'd Demand my Own Representation,
That should be in
All our Rights.

Buried Alive

Here lying in this unmarked grave rests the living
dead — choking up dirt.
Shovels
and
Shovels
of
No Substance and
Zero Matter
could bury any body before its time.

I cannot breathe — not with all this dirt.

Each time I rise
I attempt to survive —
In the underworld
of being
buried alive.

Preserved

Those who die young
Skip the Grave Mistakes,
They forego age and regrets:
And go straight to Heaven's Gate.

CHAPTER 16

SENSITIVE

Sensitive

That Dirty Hobo has been out in the cold too long...

He's Numb.

That Filthy Slut has been Slammed so many times...

She can't Feel Anything.

As the nation becomes more Politically Correct with Every Passing Year:

I guess some just aren't worth the Coverage.

American Etiquette

She sorts through her collection to find the dress...
best fitted for a lady.
Yes tonight he'll be in the company of a lady,
And she — hosted by a Gentleman.

She glides down the stairs wearing an elegant one shoulder silver sequin with diamond earrings and two-inch heels...only two inches...four and above would make him think she's a whore. No, she is a lady.

He picks her up and opens the door, as a true gentleman should. He is dressed well, and has on the finest cologne, and together they take to the city.

They go out to dinner and familiarize with one another, then prepare to enjoy their course.

Mmmm...she has the broiled spicy tofu, and he the house salad. She nibbles in a dainty fashion and he wears his napkin in his collar. He remembers to use the salad fork...

Good Lord you *have* to use the salad fork.

When the check arrives she *always* requires them to pay.

She is a *lady* and *not* a whore.

After cocktails he drops her off at her apartment and together they stroll to the door…and her gentleman accompanies her inside.

Then they Fuck like Animals.

A couple weeks go by and the contact fades.
Lack of communication and general boredom.

Anyway, he is just another in a Long Line before him who lacked enough class.
She deserves better.
Maybe someday she'll settle:
Only when she's found the Best.

Tonight she returns to the closet…
To prepare again for another fine gentlemen…
Oh but he *must* open her door:
for she is a *lady*, and *not* a whore.

Job Security + Workplace Insecurity =...

If she has provided for shelters in need — with an ungenerous salary, but a generous heart...

If she has volunteered to help many foundations — in order to rebuild a better community...

If she has selected a giving profession — in order to help touch — and heal lives...

If she has given all of herself — for every minute — of every day — long after her shift is through...

Would all that cancel out the time she posed nude in that "inappropriate" magazine?

Probably not...

That wouldn't set a good example.

Give That Man A Hand

The guy is out here trying...
More than you'll ever know...
You can't tell but he's probably dying,
So just listen before you go.

Travel-Bound citizens pretend they can't listen...so
without the aid of this noisy Red-Line Train Station:
They block out the sound of The Man with the Golden
Voice...because they're afraid
He might ask for a handout...
A little love would substitute for money...
So it's ok — gone and put your hand out.

He's broke and probably quite hungry...
But this is more than just a "pity cause..."
Just give him what he's earned,
And that's at *least* a round of applause.

I am not encouraging the donation of a dollar,
Though that would be kind, too...
I'm saying to look past his dirty wardrobe:
And Give the Man his Due.

He's jamming now but he's really down and out...
He'd appreciate change and a rousing ovation...but
he could Really use a Friendly Hand Out.

Someday *you too* may need a hug…
So let's board This Train of
Peace & Love.

You don't need to give a scrappy hand out…
To shake a hand, applaud, or
Put your Hand Out.

CHAPTER 17

ROOM AND BORED PACKAGE

Top Hat

Haven't had many Lids on me,
Since I'm working with a limited
Salary Cap,
But if I could afford a massive collection,
Then Baby, you would be my
Top Hat.

Red Light

Long-Faced Johns pull up and see a
Strawberry District.
They pedal to their destination, but soon cross the
line.
This apparent Cherry-Red District suddenly changes
to a
Flashy Red Light.

This joint leaves many a fantasy Crimsoned and
Clubbed,
They were expecting the full treatment
And only leave with a Rub.
Look Man, No Hands!
Just Look, Man, but No Hands!
She works that pole with no hands,
And If you Try to lend a helping hand:
You're lucky to
Just get banned.
If her Ass even Thinks it feels a hand,
Your Butt will
Soon get Canned.
She looks revved and ready,
So now you're geared to go,
You can tip hundreds for weeks,
And She Will Still Say, "No."

You're so blinded by her Headlights,
You can't even see the Unchanging Red Light.

Now we may have to Pay for Toll,
High Speed Makes us Pay the Cops,
Some Pay for an Open Road,
But Why Would You Pay to Stop?

Get It Off Your Chest

Eyes are the window to the soul,
Nothing could be more personal,
So when My eyes slide down Your person,
Let's just call it an Undress Rehearsal.

Let me try again!
Give me another chance!
You can't blame me for looking down!
I was mesmerized by your mammary glands!

But now I'm focused, man!
I mean, your eyes are beautiful, too...
Ah, hell, who are we really kidding?
You wore that top to show off your boobs.

Your Bodice more than complements your Body,
You point to your eyes as a clever disguise...
But don't be too offended...
It's not like my focus is between your thighs.

What'd you expect by wearing that?
Your overreaction bares a plotted test...
You can't blame my eyes for discovering gold —
And wanting to pull out your Treasure Chest.

I'll stare at your eyes,
I Guess —
If I Must...

I'll stare at the rest when you walk away,
But let's put this secret to rest:
The Whole Room would be looking if you had your way.

Snow Day

The bitterness outside is blighting,
Let's go in and play...
We'll warm up next to our Fire,
And make it a cozy
Snow Day.

Room and Bored Package

Ok, so we're not compatible.
I can see we don't share the same interests...
but what I Don't understand:
Is why that means we can't
Share the same Mattress.
If you're getting a little sleepy,
I'll give you a place to lay your head:
I don't care if
I Put you to Sleep —
As long as
I Take You to Bed.

CHAPTER 18

MODUS OPERANDI

Nurse's Orders

If I found love...I'd nurse it — no, I'd
Coach It.
No-no wait, yeah I'd nurse it.
I mean yeah there's the downsides,
The tragic accidents,
The burns,
And maybe even a train wreck or two...
But that's not really what I mean.
I was gonna say I'd coach it, but I think "nurse it" is better.
Yeah, I like that better.
Because I'd make sure that shit stays alive.
And I'd do it with tough love.
And strategy, too.
So you can understand why I was about to say "coach?"
No, but yeah, I'm sticking with nursing it.
Is that effeminate to choose nursing over coaching?
A lot of guys are nurses nowadays...

Man, I'd be a hell-of-a nurse...
Because I'd make sure it stays alive.
How?
Well I'd sort of be that Doctor of Love you always hear about.
Only I'm Only a Nurse.

I'd have irregular consults and be like,
"Baby, slow downnnnn..
I'm not going anywhere.
You got my line. I gave you my Extension."

Seems after I gave her that Extension —
My phone couldn't stop ringing.

We talked for hours just yesterday...
&
Sat under Capella in sync in A Cappella:
Just three days before tomorrow.

You need to take a break,
Otherwise you'll exhaust yourself...
Worse Yet — You'll Exhaust Us...
This Investment is gonna take Trust.
So believe me when I say I'll be here...
We've had enough memories to last a week-time...
So don't come back so soon —
Or our love will turn into a flat line.

I'm Her Type!...Ohhhh...Negative.

She thinks I got a body like Vin Diesel —

No Homo.

She thinks I'm cute like lil' Michael —

No Molester.

But I gotta see how she works up close —

Gotta Test Her.

And the results come back...

And I don't.

Modus Operandi

We can measure this moment. Put it in our lab and set aside times for mating
— But strap on gloves to avoid reproducing.
We can reheat these molecules and rekindle our body temperatures —
Downing it in swarded weed fields that we aver will rise and grow
at the first sign of moisture. Perhaps it will.
But more likely than not, we will not be able to cultivate the growth that is firmly grounded
In This Moment.

I know society and customs won't let us act now,
So when I become too forward you must back down.
But way, way, planted deep down:
You know
And
I Know:
It could never be hotter
Than if it happened in this spot.
In This Moment.

Or even just on this night.

Initial Mystery, curiosity, and spontaneous unbridled lust cannot reoccur,
It can only recycle —
And if you choose *not* to discard something in demand —
How can I call you trash?

Baby, if I didn't respect you, I wouldn't have asked you.
Or Want You.

If I wouldn't respect you, then I wouldn't respect myself.

You must respect that which mainsprings a positive response;
I feel a discharge coming tonight, and it's not your dignity.

I don't think we can bottle these hormones.
We need to hold on to it now.
Act on it now.
I want to let it flow — outside of the world's pre-programmed lab,
Still — you insist on using your stopper.

You can't record this feeling with digital data or entered numbers —
If we're lucky we can find a similar spark when we return to the lab,
but the flame we had will extinguish by an emergency procedure that you were told to carry out
by unnamed sources with white coats and beakers of wet dreams on their mantels.

If only we could have acted on impulse, instead of following procedure —

We would've burned this mother down.

CHAPTER 19

LET IT DIGEST

Have Mercy

Ok! You can take my wallet! Just please...just don't shoot!
Take the money, take the credit cards, too!
Just...just don't shoot!
Take the shoes off my feet and the clothes off my back —
I've already exposed myself anyway...
plus I'd love to bare all again.
Yeah, I know people don't want to see strangers naked, but some
may like what's *Underneath*...
Go ahead! Take it all!
Go to my house and take my TV, too!
Clean my closet, go and trash the place!
Urgghhh...fine, you can have my laptop, too.
Take whatever you want — Do what you want with me! —
Just Please —
Don't Take my Brainchild.

When you get to the house and open up that laptop,
Keep cleaning me out and the cops will not lurk,
Ok, fine! You can shoot me, too!
Just please: Do not steal my work.

That's just mean, man.

Let It Digest

I understand that there are So Many Writers and you only have so much capacity.
I realize that I'm just a dish in the larger course of contemporary literature.
I accept that you can only digest so much of me, before you leave room for all the others.
For however long you absorb these words…until you've forgotten its flavor…

I'd just like to thank you for taking this in —
And actually giving a crap.

The Gift

If I could set my own price,
I'd settle for the minimum amount,
You could just give me a penny for my thoughts:
Because it's the thought
That Counts.

LET IT DIGEST

Hang

Hang.
Don't Rush It.
That's enough for today —
Don't Push It.
Just Hang.

I'm your compliant hostage,
I'm all bound up and not going anywhere.
And there's nowhere else I'd rather be.
Don't move on so quickly.
Let's Hang.

If this will be a bookshelf companion,
We can't make this a One Night Stand.
I'd love to see you tomorrow.
We should Hang.

Put it down, Let it Marinate.
Leave it out to dry.
Or better yet:
Let it Hang.

Please Hang on Every Last Word,
because it's one more year 'til the next one drops.

CHAPTER 20

RESPECT FOR THE DEAD

Counterfeit

I was watching the Game Show Network the other day.

I'm pretty sure it was yesterday.

And there was this one contestant who had a chance to make a Million Dollars.

The problem is, she pushed her luck too far and kept going when she should have stopped.

I don't understand why they don't just take the money.

Anyway, she lost everything in an instant. She was leaving without a single penny more than what she came in with.

Now, the part I don't understand… is after she lost everything…after all her wishes crumbled…

She smiled…

She *smiled*.

She and the Game-Show host sort of took part in a little departing banter, and she left the stage…

Smiling and Waving the whole way out.

I was so fascinated that I studied her smile. I looked for any hint of phoniness to see
If the Smile was Counterfeit...and...I couldn't find it. Not a trace.
If I had just tuned in as she was exiting, I might actually think she had won something.
That is how genuine her smile looked.
But everyone knows that is impossible.
We don't really know what she is thinking or feeling.
All we see is a smile.
I thought to myself that
We cannot trust what she is showing the world
At Face Value.
Then, in that instant, I came to a realization:

I've seen that smile before.

What's Wrong With You?

Aw, you're an alright guy!
Thanks.
Thanks for caring.
I'd love to open up
and
Go ahead and let it all out.
I would.
No Really, I would.
Yeah, all of it…
I'd love to tell you about my
Disappointments,
Heartaches,
Heartaches that never were…
Whooo! Maybe that'd help, right?
That's why you asked, right?
The question? "What's wrong?"
Well, I'm so glad you care.
Tell you what, I'll make you a deal:

Let's know each other for more than ten minutes,
Now there's a novel idea!
Maybe then I'd tell you my whole life story,
Oh I can't wait! Just wait right here!
Dude, I'mma pour it all on you!
I'mma let my
Soul Glowwwww!!!
No, wait, here's an Even Better Idea:
Go play confidant with someone you actually know.

Respect for the Dead

Well Excuse Me,
Ms. Sunshine,
Not all worlds are as
Rosy as yours.
Believe it or not, somewhere there's
Stormy Weather,
Withering Fruit,
Delicate Flowers Trampled,
Shattered Earths,
Aftershocks…
Even people being put
In the Ground.

So the next time you see me at a funeral you know Nothing About,

Do not ask me why I am not smiling.

Exfoliation

Avocado concrete cream solidifies,
&
I stiffen.
I'm not Jim Carrie.
I'm not telling any jokes, nor can I smile without cracking.
This is how I depart, as it is too late to wash it off...

But I don't want anyone to see me like this.

This isn't me, don't judge me by today.
Tomorrow is a new day.
I'll mold the clay a new way.

You may recognize the same structure and shape,
but then you too will
see a brand new face.

This heavy weight I will sleep with it,
for I must wait a pre-set time to take it off...
Then tomorrow I will wash it off,
and begin anew — hoping for a much better treatment.

One never knows which mask we will grab when reaching in the drawer,
sometimes you cannot follow any recipe,
the mask forms by itself.
No, you won't see me like this.

I'll lock myself in if I have to...
I *know* I have a much, much, better face.

One of laughter & almonds, forming a cat as cool as a pair of cucumbers...
Today I'm walking on egg-shells...
I just *know* that I'm about to crack.

I do not wish this treatment on anyone, my dear,
but I do want to give you a facial.
It's a cream I'm sure you'll enjoy... one from the most natural extraction...
but today I cannot move...I am too stiff...
plus
I'm too afraid you may think that this is *always* me.
No, I'm not leaving. Not until I wash this off...
It'll be different. I will change.
This is just temporary.
You'll see.

Yes, tomorrow is a new day. The old dead skin will wash away. Then I will dig into my dark, scrambled bundle...

And hope to pull a much brighter face.

CHAPTER 21

WAITLIST

Pre-Game Show

Haven't even gone out &
My mind is on a collision,
I went from
Fyyyyrrrd Up —
to a
Game-Time Decision!
All this drinkin' and chillin'
Takes me back to my college days,
My name ain't, "Spike Lee"
But I'm still in this School Daze.
The room is already spinnin'
But let's keep these songs spinnin',
By the time we leave this room
The real party will prolly be endin'.
It's 1 AM already and our names ain't even on the list,
I might not even go out
Cuz it don't get no funner than this!
We got songs, booze and games,

So if this is just the Pre-Game:
Tonight's gonna be really special,
Hell, I'm Already glad I came.

Diamonds are Temporary, Friends are Forever

I can't calculate this change,
You were cooler as a Geek,
I understood all of your problems,
And now you're talking Greek.

You were a real chill dude
When you were one of the guys,
But you had to sell that out,
Now you're just one of the Phies.
You told me which one you joined,
But I didn't bother to remember,
Because I reminded you not to forget,
But you decided not to remember.
Oh, no, no, don't misunderstand,
This isn't another "Be Yourself" Speech,
I'm not trying to give you a lecture,
It's *Your* History I'm trying to teach.
Gone head and have a blast!
Live Your Life and Floor that Gas!
I agree — you only live once,
Just Remember the Ghosts of your Past.

You went from Bolos to Polos,
Denny Green's to Skinny Jeans,
Traded this Hearing Aid in for a Diamond…
I'll chalk that up to a Fashion Takeover,
It wasn't till you donned that Jacket —
Then I noticed an Extreme Makeover.

Waitlist

She's got so much damn class that everybody Wants In.
But she's closed off now, closed off to the world —
She ain't takin' Clothes Off — she's a Gym Class Hero.
She runs laps with those thighs over skidding eyes…
She's not ready to play with others,
So I'm stuck as her Mascot,
Now while she's playing Games —
I'm here holding my Shuttlecock.

When she's ready though, man, please, count me in!
I mean when you're ready though, woman, please, let me in!
Pick me, Pick Me! I feel you more than them all!
Now while I'm picking foes off,
She's still dodging my balls.
Seems no one else can hit her either,
They keep crossing that line,
Or maybe throwing too hard or so damn soft that she laughs.

She's got the brains to keep her bastion,
Many want to be this Beauty's Beast —
They've spent weeks exhausting their playbooks —
But can't get a Pass even with a Cheat-Sheet.

I do believe I am at an advantage:
It isn't instant gratification that I am after,

So while these inspectors try to grill her,
I have the discipline of a friar.

She's more than worth waiting for…
So while they can't even wait one year,
I could easily go another four.

Maybe it's best that she drops me,
Because I don't want to take anyone else…
And while I wait for her slot to open,
I may put my whole life on her shelf.

But the more people she turns away,
The more my odds enhance,
They run when she says, "Wait a year."
I respond, "So you're saying there's a chance?"

And if she is unexpectedly snatched up,
And extends my stay upon this Waitlist,
As long as there are stars in the sky:
She'll remain Alone atop my Wish List.

CHAPTER 22
SOMEBODY MUST HAVE DIED TONIGHT

Rock Star/Copy. Write it.

They made the music;
You Own the Moment.

Dancing in the Middle of a Nightclub

The clock just struck midnight, on a winter Sunday night.
Still, my ideas can't stop movin',
That's why I'm
Dancing in the Middle of a Nightclub.

Now who goes clubbin' on a Sunday night?
Apparently a very large crowd.
Who dances in the middle of a nightclub?
Only
Da Champ.

While everyone else tries to jot down numbers,
I'm by myself — just fine — plotting these lines.

The noise doesn't make me confused —
I use the speakers as my muse.
Tonight isn't about numbers...
Only these letters.

I'm off to the side, but hands not in my pockets —
They're holding this trusty notebook...
No numbers, ok
Maybe Just 1 —
In this
Little
Black
Book.

The Exit

Make your entrance with your own sense of style,
&
If that happens to be the same as the crowd —
Hell, that's fine, too…Just as long as it's You!

The whole universe seems to have shrunken into the size of an orb,
Which means in this room — On this Night —
You Can Be the Biggest Star in the World.

You need not be an astronomer to focus on a shine that brightens the room.
One doesn't require a flashlight, the room's a bit dark, but we can just use your spotlight —
Suddenly we can see your whole crew:
Just because they're standing with you.

Step Easy, you already shook up the room,
Now the only thing left is to
Time Your Big Boom:
The "Big Bang Theory" of going out with a Bang,
Would only Detonate that High Note you just Sang.
Soak it all In & Stay for a while…
Because once you leave this Room:

You'll Disappear Like X-Files.

Somebody Must Have Died Tonight

God...He or She must have been Really Special.
The Streets appear much Blacker than Usual.
This suited Saturday Night is dressed down to Tees & PJs —
I was fitted to go out...and now I'm wondering where everyone went.
There's barely a blazer in sight...no funeral procession, not even a Hearse...
But this grim scene is evidence enough:
Somebody Must Have Died Tonight.

Not just anybody, but Somebody.
May not have been tonight — maybe during this past week —
The name of this person may not have been well-known,
but their soul must have lit up this town.

Most think that when they die they'll
Take the world with them...

He or she was Actually Right.

CHAPTER 23

SHE CAN GROW

She Can Grow

It will not always be like this.
Believe it or not.
Yes, that nestling daisy will blossom into a bird's-foot violet.
The whole world will want to pick at her, hold her,
And gaze at her beauty.
Something so delicate must be tendered…
Nurtured and cared for with the investment of a provider and the
Medicine of a Caregiver.
Yes, she needs you to be raised.
But She Can Grow.

She can manage her own Garden…
With Only the Nourishment of Nature — She Can Bloom,
She Can Grow.

What could result may be callous and harsh,
Or might remain untarnished as larch,
Whatever produces is in the roots of Her Nature…

You will not give her away to the world:
The World Will Take Her.
What She Gives Them is Up to Her.

Your flower may get ruined and damaged,
Or may remain up-kept and managed,

What's in her Nature:
Only She Knows...
She Will Live.
She Will Grow.

Letting Go

Whenever I hugged my mother as a child,
The hardest part was
Letting Go.

And when 10 year reunions are formed
or a spouse returns home from a long day,
or a child, not unlike me, hugs his mother,
They Too must eventually let go.
It's that "Let Go Moment" when the amount of seconds add up to a magic moment, and once it is felt, it's ok: you can let go. Even if you want to hold on forever, you force yourself to let go…and sometimes after a few short seconds, the magic returns, and you hug again.

They hold one another by the sleeve,
They stare, and my word
They Smile.
They may hug over and over again, but sooner or later, they must
Let Go.

I always hated to let go.

Mothers, most of all, fear letting go.

As I unloaded our van into my dorm room,
I noticed a proud, yet sorrowful mother…

She held her daughter for 18 years...

And as a tear fell,
She waved
&
Let Go.

Modest Girl in a Fast Life

She'd rather stay in tonight,
but she doesn't really have a choice.
She likes to read, write, draw…spend time
With the family…
She's been a simple girl all her life…
but the world would have nothing of it…
Now she's a Modest Girl in a Fast Life.

Other girls want her in their pack…and guys just want her…
The most cloistered and private spirit cannot hold in beauty…
&
Her genial ways make it even harder for her to resist the inevitable:
She's a Modest Girl stuck in a Fast Life.

She does not get around,
and someday she'll make the
Perfect Wife…
Until then her time's
Not hers to give —
She's a
Modest Girl in a Fast Life.

CHAPTER 24

SCENIC VIEW

Apologizing for Defacing Angels

I'm sorry,
I thought it was the
Heart of a Dove
and the
touch of lax linen
That makes an angel.
I'm sorry,
I *still* say that Angels
have an Inner Grace
that goes Much Deeper
than the face.

Scenic View

I won't be getting too far,
All your signs have made that clear.
I'm telling myself to pump the brakes, but
I just want to look a little bit longer.

I'm taking in clouds of rippled islands floating above wide open pineries and mellow-high forests with trees & leaves as green as Irish cress. Clear postmeridian sunshine belight my path like candle-light in a dead cave. I see beyond the fact that we're going nowhere. I see beauty. Deep, Natural Beauty.

Pull over, let me look at you.

I'm not stopping,
But I'm not ready to move on.

Stop running, let me look at you.

Let me take in sky-honey fantasies with rolled down windows on either side of me. Slick Breezes skip on my skin...they groove my jagged edges to a better place — at a slow pace. I'm easing down this one-way street because I already know what's waiting for me on the other side. Which is why as you're avoiding looking at your latest roadkill that you never meant to hurt, I'm looking right at your cool western hills. I'm tired of trying to climb the insurmountable. I'll just park right here and stare in admiration. It was a nice day out, but now it just got beautiful. This lonely road is now beaconed in gold — from a sun that shines all-throughout you.

This road is going Nowhere,
When I had hoped
It would lead to you...
I'm still going down this
Dead End Street:
Because I'm Enjoying the
Scenic View.

Imagine

I see an Iris Blossom,
Instead of a
Venus Flytrap.
I capture a Meteoric Rise,
Instead of
Hanging on a falling star.
I already feel Sunbursts,
Instead of
Solar Winds.
I notice a New Moon,
Instead of
Paralyzing Gravity.
I marvel at a Green Ray,
Instead of Running from
A Thundercloud.
I refresh at First Light,
Instead of remaining with Twilight.
I imagine the South Pacific —
Instead of a
Frozen Lagoon.
I imagine Fair View Mountain,
Instead of another
Continental Slope.
I imagine parachuting Snow Mist,
Instead of a
Tumbling Avalanche.
I imagine casing a Sapphire,
Instead of
Pawning a Pinchbeck Pearl.

Now Imagine how I'd feel if it became a reality.

Don't listen to the cynics and pessimists,
I'd change quite a bit for you...
I'd get on up off this bed,
And earn a King's Ransom to lay our heads.
I don't know what the future holds,
I doubt you'll even know my full thoughts,
I'm just saying that if you Did have me —
You'd change quite a few of my faults.
These cynics say that women make the mistake —
Of thinking they can change a man...
I've made enough mistakes for us both,
So trust me when I say that you can.

If they are referring to thugs and criminals,
And I should ever convert to that type:
I'd soon match your white — and quickly shed old stripes.

They keep on giving that advice,
But think again before you
Take it as True...
These People — They Don't Know Me,
And they Sure as Hell must not know You.

CHAPTER 25

UNDER THE TABLE

Politics

I call it straight down.
Tell it like it is.
If I tell you something will happen:
You can put it on your kids.
I won't kiss your babies,
I won't wave or smile at the podium,

But when I stand up here I'll *always* tell you the truth,
Tell me the truth:
How many others can say that?

I won't campaign for your votes,
I will be exactly who I am:
I *refuse* to play your game,
You can leave your politics to Uncle Sam.

If wearing a minstrel smile is the way to get ahead:
Then I'd rather work the fields instead.

So you can keep your jobs, networks, and parties...
I can write my own ticket...
I won't smile for your Political Parties,
I will build my own damn picket.

At Your Service

They may throw out your App,
Could always dock your pay...
But your identity is Yours,
Don't let them take it away.
These pleas you do not heed,
They bought a new machine,
Don't speak to me like a Robot,
You're still a Human Being.

The Receipt

Do you want your receipt?

Wait, don't answer that.
Just take it, bitch.

You've had it coming for
Way too long and I've come a long way to give it to you.
I'd think twice about putting up too much a fight if I were you...
Just take it.

You've wronged the wrong one —
Now I'm back with the vengeance of a grieving son.
What do you get when you cross me then I cross you *out?*
Payback.

It's written on the paper that I vowed to serve up.
It has the vows of my revenge pledge that I swore to uphold,
I waited on purpose
cuz
It is best served cold.

But if you thought I'd cool off you're about to be dead wrong...
I hope you told your folks what's your favorite song.
That apostrophe ain't for

"is"...
you're about to be a
"was,"
Afterwards I'll piss on your grave —
Just Because.

My words cut like the blade of a "Hattori Hanzo" sword,
And my wrath cuts to the bone like a dagger-laced cord....
So while you're in pieces from being cut up,
I'll be in pieces and
Cutting Up.

lmao.

I don't dance so I'll settle for a victory laugh,
In my lesson on revenge —
I'll explain using math:

The addition of my infliction added up his attrition —
I solved my conflict with a
Word Problem:

You remember what you get when the wrong one is crossed then the two cross paths again...and only one walks away?

Evidence that someone has Successfully Paid.

Mother Fucker I Left the Receipt.

Uhhh...

Angry Boss: "I don't pay you to think!"
Employee: "Uhhh....I thought you did..."

Under the Table

Didn't you know?

You have to have a D Cup to Pour Drinks,
or at least be
Too Hot to Handle.
Yeah...
And if you wanna sell merchandise, then
You better have the Goods,
and you can't just tell about the offer, you
Gotta
Show 'Em What You Got...
Seems if you're not Working with Something then you'll probably
be
Working for next to Nothing.

I'm just informing you about the ways of business:
They don't think they'll make a Fraction: Without a Main Attraction.
But now that can't be, can it?
We wouldn't drink less just because her top shows less,
We'd still get Tanked even if her face looked Pranked...
And I came in just for the Wings!
Not cuz I wanna add Breasts.

Now I'm not Sayin' I won't look —
Just That Food was all it took.

Wish I could say this was just for overnight sensations
With misguided hopes of undercover relations,
But it seems the same applies to every field of taxations —
Sometimes even more than gigs *without* Taxation...
A degree might not be enough if you want to be on top,
Sometimes it takes being on bottom to be directed to the top...
Seems I can't find a woman in a suit that I don't want to tear out of —
You should be able to be a little overweight and still Wait,
Still expect a lot of tips without being granted tits...
And be a little full and still have some pull...
Excuse Me. Can I please get a casual face?
Or see someone get hired without an ass like a vase?
Well all the "real" women now are probably sitting behind desks:
If she's only taking calls then we can pretend it's Jessica Hall.
And right when they find their sanctuary —
They're bumped for a hot new secretary.

I tell you if Jill Scott and Kelly Price can sell as modeled,
Then you gotta figure if they had a slimmer figure
They'd be making over Eight Figures.
They may be lucky they even got in, because someone surely said to them,

"You're too big to Fit In."
Every day a deserving Executive is turned into a Fry Lady,
If you got a Hatchet-Face then they make you a Crybaby.
The Fairer Sex has been treated Way too Wrong,
Debarred from Equal Opportunity against
Their Own too Long,
It's gonna take a Strong Man
To come and
Right this Wrong,
Or a Natural Woman like Aretha
To sing a Shaping Song...
Until then I'll take my service to whoever fills my needs,
That doesn't change if she's a Sprig or she has Double-Ds...
And I don't tip for the cleavage — I'll tip for the Deeds —
You shouldn't have to hit your knees to hear a simple, "Yes, Please."

CHAPTER 26

SCARS

Martyr

Freedom doesn't come easy.
Someone inevitably must suffer for it.
If everyone could be happy —
"Happy" would just be "Content."
If that's the price to pay for others' happiness,
I shall reluctantly step forward…
I may not be reaping the benefits,
but I'm hoping someone will
Pay it Forward.

It's mostly not my choice.
I was selected from the masses
to
Endure psycho-physical torment while excruciatingly resisting tears
in a cycle of water-torture most commoners could never withstand.
I have been pushed to the brink and tested again and again…

but
I Will Not Break.
So I will bravely continue to bear the bondage and go on to suffer the lashes of these Vicious Whips.

I Will Not Beg for Mercy,
I'll Only
Prepare to be Stricken Harder:
"It is the Cause and not the Death" —
This is the
Mantra
Of
A Martyr.

Scars

Warriors display their scars —
The same scars that left them exposed —
Vulnerable & Naked.
Scars that remain Unhealed…
Only Palliated — And
No Longer Noticeable.
Fresh scars don't bleed smiles
& Attractions.
You host a merry-go round of "Show and Tell…"
You've become fond of saying, "Show me yours and I'll show you mine."
You've survived battles and wars of words and cataclysmic explosions brought about by shadowed ambushes of trust and fidelity.
You are a Survivor.
And Damnit — you want the world to know it.
You are still standing, and you are undaunted in the face of stepping out into the battlefield once more — and moreover — again and again. Though every now and then…
You flinch at the flash of another ambush.

Even the Bravest Soldier is secretly a little bit afraid.

I cannot remove my armor,
I've become far too accustomed to carrying it.
You've already shown me your collection.
You describe how much they hurt when fresh and how long you've carried them…

How do you think it feels to not have a mark?
I'd swear I'm twice as wounded as you —
But I don't have the scars to prove it.

You've been hit head on after an enduring engagement,
All I have are
Glancing Blows
from
Cold Wars.

I'd swear I'm twice as wounded as you —
But I don't have the scars to prove it.

You expose because you feel like a Survivor,
I guard with the reflex of a chronic casualty.
The recoil of rejection stings like hell —
And makes you feel like you're ill-equipped.

I'd swear I'm twice as wounded as you —
But I don't have the scars to prove it.

When you lure me into the battlefield,
Trust that I am more than ready for contact.
Afterwards you can display your scars as you've done with the others,
but don't wait for me to follow your lead.

I understand you're used to trading war stories,
Yet I'll still hold my heart to my chest,

Though you have more badges on record,
Seems I'm the only one with Post-Traumatic Stress.

I Swear I'm Twice as Wounded As You.

You claim to be battle-scarred,
Yet the words seem to flow on out...
It is much harder to Open Up:
When there is Nothing to Open Up
About.

CHAPTER 27

IN THIS CAGE LIES A BEAST

Unbalanced

I've slipped up.
Maybe I didn't step hard enough.

Maybe I didn't call enough.
Could have taken her to better places.
Despite my strong chances —
I Slipped, Fell, and Failed.

This dogged lack of experience
Has regenerated an underworld of inexperience.

Don't think I didn't want you,
I tried my best to do you good...
I Swear:
There's more to what you didn't see,
I Would Have Done Better —
If I Could.

His-Pussy

It's me, it's not you — That's the truth.
Everybody has a history,
Just that some are harder to accept than others.
To you it might be *ancient* history,
but to me I Still see the "others."

Only a fool would judge you for having a life,
Living a Past,
Being Human.
But that expired certificate still means something.
Maybe not to you or him...but to me.
And when I picture him dropping off your kids and driving off for months at a time...he may as well have a tattoo down there that says, "OWNED."
They're beautiful,
So are you...
But while you say, "History,"
I just hear, "His-Pussy."

In this Cage Lies a Beast

I've been in this cage for well over ten years.

I wish I could say I haven't been rattled.

I would roam as a young panther on my way to prowling for bobcats when I would become a dashing jaguar.

I enjoyed these tender years where the only thing I needed to attack was the scene.
Someone so wild and ferocious was to no danger to those at large — rather, he was the life of parties, and a sharp shooter at the art of ranging.
Oh, I was fierce alright. But I was harmless.

Still —

They Caged Me Anyway.

When whirling bullets and gangs of wandering vultures couldn't keep me in —
All it took was spaces just a little bit too open — to lock away liberation — and preserve inhibitions.

I have been let out every now and then. If I looked hard enough, I may have even found traces of the self that came before myself and spots of the cat that wouldn't shy from running with big dogs or going up a class in a combat without eight lives to fall back on. The combat was bloodless, but ask anyone and they'll tell you: it's cutthroat. I was prepared to embrace danger if it meant remaining free and part of a community, yet instead of licking my chops and stepping right back out into the wild — I was far too domesticated — far too soon.

I showed all the promise of a young lion, but I will never know what adventures may have lie ahead of me: for I have been in this cage for most of my adult life.

Instead of roaring, I whisper. Instead of shouting cries, I stifle tears. This domestic life appears more polished and furnished, but when you step out and there is nowhere to go, it is only then when you realize how wide those bars extend and before you know it, the whole world becomes your cage. I may appear primed and feral upon first sight, but there are some things you just cannot see: In this Beast lies a Cage.

Try and try, but I can't break free.

Sometimes,

All it takes is a full moon and some spirits, and something comes over me.
If I'm lucky —
Just a little moonlight and some moxie will be more than enough.

In a matter of weeks, days, or often as soon as when the next sun comes up, I'll return to form.

But on that night, there is no controlling the animal. For my nature may seem reclusive, but look again — for it is only a cage. And In This Cage Lies a Beast. My true nature is the one I was born with. The one that was embedded in me. You can de-nurture and expose to mental torture, and you can take the animal out of the wild, but there will always remain a little bite.

I will lure bobcats I never got to chase, I will dance with cougars and flirtatious felines and I will rise above the competition of other hunters. And if this impending drinking binge qualifies as a war game:

You will not be the one left standing.

The crowd usually closes in on me...
But tonight: I won't be the one to stray.
Tonight, I am thrilled to be let out - - -

And

I don't ever want to go back.

While these nights appear revisitable,
I can redo everything the exact same way tomorrow —
And not feel the slightest bit free.

So tonight I will release upon release —
And go in for the kill before this moment dies.

The person you were expecting may not show up.
When it is confirmed that he has surfaced — look closer.

When I appear aloof and remote,
And you move in to gently pet this hushed creature you thought you knew —

Beware.

CHAPTER 28

INSIDE IN THE NOVEMBER RAIN

Rasslin Lingo

I was naïve to everything you did,
That's called a "Mark."
Some just go along even though they know better,
That's called a "Smart Mark."
Other people are just plain cynical,
These are called the "Smarks."

The smarks are a little obnoxious,
Nothing is stopping them from walking away,
Though they keep right on complaining...
They end up watching again anyway.

The Smart Marks are the perfect blend,
They can suspend their awareness for illusion,
When the show is over they can pick it apart,
It's a weekly psychogenic transfusion.

I loved it most when I was a mark,
When I believed it All was real:

From "Macho Man" to Jake the Snake —
Even George "The Animal" Steele.

You see as a mark I had an advantage,
I could lose myself inside those characters,
But as you grow older you stop being naïve,
And it is no different than with you and me.

I believed every word you told me —
I was a Mark for Heaven's Sake!
I used to stare with a child's admiration,
Even though deep down I knew it was fake.

Those days are over now,
You made too many high-risk maneuvers: Now your backstage secrets are revealed.

Today I consider myself a Smart Mark,
I know the difference between real and fake...
Though I still love watching you:
I'm analyzing every move that you make.

Inside in the November Rain

Yesterday was a night called "Black Wednesday."
Tomorrow is known as "Black Friday."
Today I should be out Celebrating,
But I refuse to discover "Black Thursday."

Today is 11/25,
Exactly 5 months to the day,
Though I haven't had much to be thankful for,
I'm still Celebrating the Greatest Art —
After All.

It is the art that composes me,
When in the past — I would have been viral,
I've found that there is always an upside —
To lift me up amid a Downward Spiral.

Who knows what tomorrow brings?
Maybe the rain will begin to fall again...
But today like many weeks before it —
I've grown to love these ruffled shoes I'm in.

It isn't thanks to dated clichés
Such as, "It could always be worse..."
I was feeling bad enough as it was,
but decided
Hope, Peace and Love
Come First.

Hope comes with every breath that I draw,
Peace is an inner trans-movement,
My love is bottled in as its companion —
So it leaks from every word that I sketch.

Millions of gathering loved ones prepare to feast as this clock strikes Noon,
While my room and table remain empty,
My stomach sits still —
It's still early; I know I'll eat later...
"Mother Fate" will fill me up,

Even though most have already eaten.

Go ahead and "gobble till you wobble,"
And while you're filling your apparatus,
I'm here laughing at that goofy status.

Hell, it's still a good feeling.

As I dine alone to a parade of games,
Outside there is a crowd of cheers...
Somewhere out there is an Antwone Fisher,
Who in this moment is Moved to Tears.

That to me is a Cause for Celebration.

This weary, grey Autumn sky
Forebodes a Sanguine day of Conviviality
With tangelo and pumpkin leaves
being shed from this reposed

Tree of Harvest
with Mandarin stuffed felicity and Cranberry dewdrops
In an Outpouring of Affection.
Only a few miles away but still back from a Leave of Absence.
Go on in, take your coat off,
Check the problems of the year at the door.

I'll be Inside in the November Rain,
Suiting up for a frigid December,
And think back on this year and my life,
To make this a November to Remember.

I play the ballad by Guns N' Roses,
With ECW making the tunes contextual,
Been doing it since '98,
It's my own Annual Ritual.

As another year winds down,
I know not what the next one holds,
But I *will* stand firm,
Prepared for Whatever Unfolds.

I'll Keep Getting Up Until I'm Full,
But Never Settle for Seconds.

I gave up on giving up,
I'll keep on thinking lofty…
I Quit being a Cold Turkey,
And turned into a Big Softy.

I believe in unrealistic dreams,
I grin at the corniest jokes,
I still believe in Miracles and Angels,
Despite reality's relentless pokes.
I fear I will again awake
To the Cold Rain of The Pain that was Streaming,
Yes, I Know Nothing Lasts Forever,
So Let Me Keep on Dreaming.

* * *

Next Year, just like Today,
I'll Just Be Thankful for Being Here.

CHAPTER 29

FREE COUNTRY

Colors

Didn't realize it took the same Ethnicity
To Have Some Fun,
I'll Embrace
Any Color
That
Does Not Run.

Free Country

I stood as firm as
Malcolm X.
I swore not a one of them was good.
Went Out of My Way to Distance Myself.
But then — I went on a Pilgrimage.
And came back a changed man.
It took the courage of Darius Rucker and Charlie Pride…
but
I now see good or bad can be found in everything.
I can change my mind — It's a Free Country.

I was convinced no good could be found,
It took only one song to turn that notion around:
Tim McGraw's Plea to not "Take the Girl,"
Was the first step into a closed off world.
Within a year's time I came to find more good than I allowed myself to ever consider was out there…
Now I'm free to travel with the Chrome of Trace Adkins,
Bounce on the waves of Randy Travis' voice up to Sugarland…
Though it seems some people wouldn't understand.
If one sat down and objectively listened to the mind-gaping voices of Carrie and Martina or
the seraphic sound of Allison Kraus…you may have the same revelation as I did.
With respect to the pioneers like Haggard and Brooks,

It was the Belles like LeAnn Rimes that showed
me the Big Deal — and Women like Wynonna who
Came from the Heart like Kathy Mattea that took me
further than Dixie — But those are my Chicks, too.
Are some as rotten as I initially thought?
I suppose.
But I now see the truth past what people have been
whispering in my ears —
There is good in Everything.

Quite a bit I can still do without,
I may Pass on Alabama and Big Country,
But I can go wherever I choose:
And keep enjoying this Free Country.

CHAPTER 30

RIDE LIKE AN EAGLE

I Can Drive to the Moon

Sheer Will can take you very far.
You might be surprised.
That's how I've made it This far.
And that's how I keep on going.
Sometimes I think I want it the most…
Or at least more than most.
And as much as I want to believe otherwise —
I think the difference is who Pays the most.
If it was who wants it the most,
The Kardashians wouldn't have a best-seller…
I always have the eeriest hunch:
That the best books ever are bottom-dwellers.

Well, I might not get a lot of votes or have 100 spokes,
But I can push this thing as far as it'll go…
I just fear that when I make it to the nearest station:
The ones who pump me won't be enough.

All the compliments in the world are great,
But without something fluid it'll be too late.

I am not ready to stop,
Just give me some fuel and I'll
Get Right Back on Task.
I know I can
Drive to the Moon:
I just need a Little Gas.

The Ride

Climb on in.
You never know who might join us.
I'd love to introduce you to the band —
But I'm afraid I might leave someone out.
All you need to know is the Speakers.
That's our tour guide.
And he's a Blast.
I've wanted someone in that seat my entire life.
You don't even have to come in for me —
Just do it for the music.
Go On...Hop on in...
"Come on Baby....Don't Say Maybe."

Bumps along the way — we'll take it in stride,
So come on in and
Enjoy the Ride.

Ride Like An Eagle

I want to soar over that star-lit desert.
I want to ascend above those moss-covered trees.
But no one can fly quite like you,
So I let you take the wheel.

You turn another Lonesome Highway,
Into a scenic Seven Bridge Road,
When my gear is on cruise control —
You give me the wings to Ride Like an Eagle.

We are birds of the same feather,
Your well-traveled station channels our harmony.
If I had the freedom I'd show off your beauty —
And show how your colors move me.

I'd then tell how they speak to me —
But I can only speak for me...
Title 17501 won't let me speak for you —
So I'll be by your side enjoying this *Scenic View*

You managed to replicate my life,
I'd only like to replicate your words,
It's a small way to pay you back —
But I know that I would have to pay for that.

Instead I'll reroute this journey,
And keep you behind the wheel,
And tell of where you've taken me —
During this Long Road Out of Eden.

I held the volcano of the Flamingo
In the Palms of my hands,
You gave me the Treasure of homing in Convocation —
Airing above the Encore of being an Island.

Never has a Mirage felt so Grand,
I know one turn of the key would blow out this Palace.
I don't need to go to Paris to feel Royale —
On your wings I can fly from a shivering N-N-New York N-N-New York —
Into the Golden Sands of an Imperial Sahara.

I too have met the Ghost of Caesar
On my way to Mandalay...
It wasn't until my soul stripped on the Boulevard —
That I could fully feel all sensations stray.

Off to the side I stood,
Leaned against the glass entrance of a closed souvenir shop.
Shaded by the hushed moonlight,
With the mezzo forte radio tune airing above me.
The fast lane of the wheelin' day behind me,
I uncoiled into A Peaceful Easy Feeling.

At the shop I swapped
One Paradise for Another,
As for over four minutes my mind took off...
And gave flight to a flock of memories.

Fortunate enough to stand there from the first note,
I could recite the words with my eyes
Squinted
Closed
Open
Squinted
Absent

I could see those Diamond Earrings,
but my imagination blurred this desert of a billion stars.
I'd love to make love to someone in this Desert —
But with my eyes squinted,
I remained
Lost...
Wandering In this Peaceful Easy Feeling.

I had already flown away to this retreat,
Now I had to get away during this getaway,
After these four minutes were up,
I'd be right back on my way.

Back to looking for action.
Back to rolling for that hot hand.
Back to traipsing like a Vagrant.
I know it will be over in a flash —
Yet this feels just like home.

My room was currently empty,
Yet my sign said, "Do Not Disturb."

I know all too well what a woman can do to your soul,
Traces of their heels linger in my tenor,
That's why when I sing along to this song,
The emotion in my voice is co-attributed to her…
Some of her,
A whole lot of her…
And
<smh>
Every Last Inch of Her.

It's funny how you cash out to escape,
And the smallest thing can take you right back home,
To a time where you wouldn't be anywhere else —
But alone in a car with this same Easy Feeling.

I traveled back to the times where we "weaved down the American Highway,"
With our music blasting on a "bright and sunny day,"
Yeah we rolled down that Interstate —
Traveled the whole good ol' US of A —
During 15 minute trips to Family Video.

That's why this Desert feels so familiar,
With you as my pilot I've been everywhere…
From Egypt and Hollywood to at least two far out Circuses,
With the small charge of a CD as my air fare.

I've been that New Kid in Town,
But never a Johnny Come Lately,

Made a High School Musical of being incognito,
Figured I had my whole life ahead to grow.

The only thing that grew was this gash —
With shovels of heartbreak dressing the wound...
My seeds do not mix well with this earth —
My dusty package reads, "Cannot Bloom."

There's Gonna be a Heartache Tonight
I Know.

As long as I'm in this early grave —
There's still one more Hole in the World Tonight.

I've been clouded by fears and sorrows
with inward pleas of someone nursing this heart
tomorrow.
I sometimes blame the haunting faces of yesterday —
For letting this Hole Stay in the World today.

Funny thing about holes - -
Nobody can find you
If you don't reach out...

So I'll live with this Hole Tomorrow.

Ride Like An Eagle Pt.2/It Only Takes One Time

Switching emotions quicker than a toper switches lanes,
I Stay on Course —
With these Classic Four Wheels
I can rise above this turbulent sea.

As long as I'm in the passenger seat,
I can Ride while Under the Influence.
Intoxicated by the Fumes of Hope
&
The Sediments of Sylphs.

I can share your struggle,
Fight the very same Fight,
And Keep on Believing —
That I'll Find Her One of These Nights.
Dead On
Word for Word:
Searching for Satan's Little Girl.
Searching for that Angel in White.

Would love a Wickedly Nice Combination...
I Feel Her Out There, Too...
Nope —
Nowhere in Sight.

Still Ridin' Shotgun,
Now Looking to Nail my Prey...

No matter how many times I shoot —
I keep drawing blanks.

It Only Takes One Time

Club Hoppin'
Heart Hoppin'
Fast Stoppin'
That's alright.

I Swear I'm Gonna Find Her One of These Nights.

It Only Takes One Time

Yearning
Loneliness
Subjected to tales of romance
&
The defeating of odds too great
to overcome oneself.
Pattern Rejection
Frustration
Hopelessness
Love:
It Only Takes One Time

Ride Like An Eagle Pt.3

Still Shotgun Strapped,
But not Buckled In.
Going too fast,
Gotta slow down,
Tap that gas
&
Take It Easy.

Wind blowing against my head,
Soft-Pedaling into a waltzing Breeze
Tickling the keys of my face - -
You took me from
Huachuca to Winslow
Without a 3 Day Pass.
My trigger finger locked on repeat —
One push is all it took to stamp my ticket to freedom.
More than Seven Women on My Mind - -
Full Army — None of which on this Base —
None of them in my Company.

I can work them down to Seven
And even cast the parts of the
Four,
The Two, and the
Friend of Mine.
I want to keep moving down the road,
Hitchhike into the Backseat of a Queen's Creek,
And Kick Start my Heart down to Winona.

I'm still waiting for your sweet love to
come and save me.

Lamentation has never felt so Tranquil.
I can ride the waves of these flowing tunes
Halting these constantly Spinning Wheels
from Driving me Crazy.

I'm Easy.

Ride Like an Eagle Pt. 4/Fences

You completed the manuscript of my life,
Before I was even born.
It touches and resonates with Millions
Without tarnishing the eerie copy of my version.
You composed it better than I ever could —
Taking Commuters to a Deep Introspection.
You provide a setting of an Inward Nature —
I see New Mexico and the Mountains of Colorado,
It gives new hope to love's Obstinate Outlaws,
No Longer a Rider - - I'm a Desperado.

Can't Paraphrase,
Count me in with the Others —
Word
For
Word
This is My Story, Too.

* * *

My gates wouldn't let them pass,
I turned the masses to "denses..."
Just throw one more curve my way...
&
I swear — I'll Swing for the Fences.

* * *

My eyes re-open as they begin another tune,
I walk away from the glass and return to the Boulevard.
Still alone at the end of this evening,
Among clusters of tourists and pros,
I Walk Alone.
I've Always Dreamt of Life in the Fast Lane,
This trip is the next best thing.
It's never too late to win the proverbial Race called Life —
So I still might get there in The Long Run.
None of these bright lights can show what's inside,
There are observers, there are doers, and there are Dreamers...
I've Always Been a Dreamer.

Yes, I dream of that woman out there
Who would've loved me —
That I never knew.
And If I should find you...then

  I'm Gonna Love You...Like Nobody's Loved You.

Until then, Strap me in,
And turn that radio on.
Keep me on that Highway.
Give me yet another sign.
You've maxed out the miles on my emotional tank,
But I'm willing to Take it to the Limit
One More Time.

When I board on the return flight back home,
And regrettably return to silence,
I'll remember that it was a Long Road Out of Eden,
but I know I can saddle up and Ride in the Sky again.
This destination can't be found in an itinerary.
A whole world is always booked and waiting...
Right inside my

Headphones

***

I'm Already Gone.

THE END :\

IMAGES

(To see each image in this book as well as other great works by these artists in FULL COLOR, please visit their great websites!!!!)

Lady Justice by Yashmin Campagne............................viii.
Artist's Website: www.yashmincampagneart.com

The Look of Love by Dian Bernardo..............................ix.
Artist's Website: www.paintingsilove.com/artist/dianbernardo

Levitation by Vincent Cacciotti......................................xii.
Copyright © Vincent Cacciotti 2011, All Rights Reserved.
www.vincentcacciotti.com

On a Hot Tin Roof by Vincent Cacciotti.........................xiii.
Copyright © Vincent Cacciotti 2011, All Rights Reserved.
www.vincentcacciotti.com

No Answer by Chet Davis..xvi.
Artist's Website: www.artsites.org/ChetDavis

ART OF MIND II: ALL IN

Wantoness by Vincent Cacciotti..xvii
Copyright © Vincent Cacciotti 2011, All Rights Reserved.
www.vincentcacciotti.com

The Door by Aixa Oliveras..xx
Artist's Website: aixaoliveras.artspan.com

Love Song by Minako Ota..xxi
Artist's Website: www.minako-art.com

Central Park South by Bruce Braithwaite....................xxiv
Artist's Website: www.brucebraithwaitestudio.com

Rainy Romp by Chet Davis..xxv
Artist's Website: www.artsites.org/ChetDavis

Box of Cretaceous by Vincent Cacciotti.........................xxviii
Copyright © Vincent Cacciotti 2011, All Rights Reserved.
www.vincentcacciotti.com

Crimson Ballerina by Kate Owens...............................xxix
Artist's Website: www.kateowensstudio.com

Tyson by Luis Ludzska..21
Artist's Website: http://luis-ludzska.artistwebsites.com/

Cell Cells by Chet Davis..57
Artist's Website: www.artsites.org/ChetDavis

Chicago River by Eric Palson......................................139
Artist's Website: www.ericpalson.com

Topless Go Go Girls by Cynthia McBride.......................145
Artist's Website: www.hillismcbride.com

Rounding the Bend by Bonnie Shapiro..........................151
Artist's Website: www.bonnieshapiro.artspan.com

Headphones by Robert Beck...208
Artist's Website: www.robertbeck.net

Each image was granted with the full written consent and permission of the artists. All rights of the images belong to the painter of each respective image.

Websites for "Art of Mind: Philosopoems to the World" Artists
(Including the great paintings from "Art of Mind: Philosopoems to the World" and other great paintings by these artists in FULL COLOR) In Order of Appearance:

Donna Marsh: dmarsh.artspan.com
Judy Gilbert: http://www.creativitymindset.net/
Chet Davis: www.artsites.org/ChetDavis
John Penney: http://www.artistjohn.co.uk/

Juliette Caron: www.juliettecaron.com
Debi Watson: www.debiwatson.com
Daniel Colvin: www.colvinart.com
Joe Cartwright: www.joecartwright.com.au/
Lori Pratico: www.loripratico.com
Kari Tirrell: www.karitirrell.com

ART OF MIND II: ALL IN

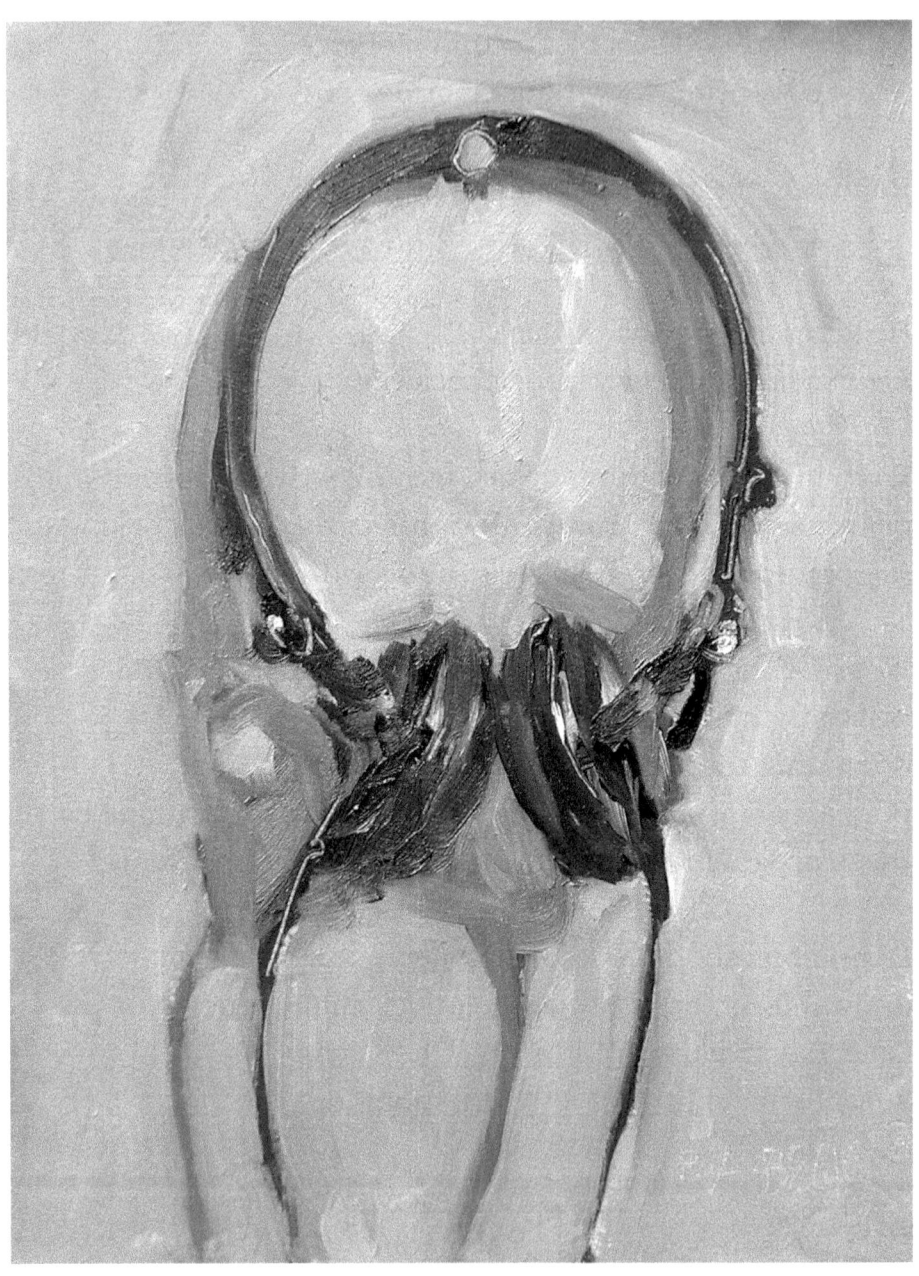

www.ingramcontent.com/pod-product-compliance
Lightning Source LLC
Chambersburg PA
CBHW071451040426
42444CB00008B/1287